SimpleWorkbooks

# Simple Estate Organizer

## A Simple System for Organizing Your Most Important Records

- Organize your important information
- Keep it all in one place.
- Have access to your documents makes decisions easier.
- Ease the transition for spouses, children and any other heirs without unnecessary confusion.

Vern Henifin of Northwest Financial Solutions
14050 SW Pacific Hwy, Suite 212, Tigard OR 97224
Phone 503-601-3272   Email vhenifin@cfiemail.com

**Vernon L. Henifin, LUTCF**

**Financial Planner**

Vern has over 35 years of experience in life, disability and health products, covering areas of retirement planning, estate planning, charitable giving, business insurance and corporate pension plans.

Vern has earned the LUTCF (Life Underwriters Training Council Fellowship) designations, and is licensed for Life, Health, Disability, Long Term Care, Fixed Annuities, Property and Casualty Insurance. He is also licensed to sell Mutual Funds, IRAs, 401K's, Variable Life Insurance, Variable Annuities Real Estate Investment Trusts, Business Development Companies and professional money management services.

He has conducted numerous seminars on wealth accumulation, retirement planning and tax strategies.

Vern resides in Tigard, Or with his wife Sharon who is the co-founder of the non-profit Breast Friends, www.breastfriends.org. Outside of work, Vern enjoys outdoor activities with his wife such as golf, fishing and hunting. Vern also loves to travel, read and build computers.

*Preface*

Northwest Financial Solutions helps individuals realize their financial needs and retirement goals. Many of our clients have had difficulty finding, or keeping their important documents organized for themselves and their loved ones.

We have put this organizer together especially for you to protect your important information and to keep it all in one place. Having access to all your documents will make your decisions easier. It will be much simpler to see the holes in your plans and help you move closer to your long-term goals. It will moreover ease the transition for spouses, children and any other heirs from the unnecessary confusion around end of life issues.

Please take some time and fill out the following questionnaire and follow the directions to complete the organizer.

Securities and advisory services offered through Centaurus Financial Inc., a registered broker-dealer and investment advisor. Member FINRA /SIPC Northwest Financial Solutions and Centaurus Financial, Inc. are not affiliated companies.

## Estate Organize Instructions

Please take some time and fill out the following questionnaire and follow the four easy steps to complete your Estate Organizer.

1. Check all boxes that apply to your individual situation.

2. Proceed to corresponding sections to fill in your details.

3. Collect all documents mentioned and place with the organizer.

   a. If your organizer is printed, place these documents with your other important papers.

   b. If you keep it in its electronic form, put your documents in one place and mention that location in your letter.

4. Create letter from template and mail to all who need this information in case of emergency.

The organizer can be placed in a notebook or roll it up and put it in your safe or safe deposit box at your bank. Either way, make sure you tell the people who need to know. Tell them that you have written all these important and helpful items down and where you have placed them for their safe keeping.

# Organizer Checklist

## 1) Personal Information

☐Yes ☐No        Family Telephone Numbers & Addresses
☐Yes ☐No        Medical Issues
☐Yes ☐No        Certified Public Accountant
☐Yes ☐No        Physicians
☐Yes ☐No        Attorney
☐Yes ☐No        Automobiles
☐Yes ☐No        Prenuptial Agreement
☐Yes ☐No        Memberships
☐Yes ☐No        Vacation Clubs/Timeshares
☐Yes ☐No        Other

## 2) Bank Information

☐Yes ☐No        Checking
☐Yes ☐No        Saving
☐Yes ☐No        Credit Cards
☐Yes ☐No        Safety Deposit Box
☐Yes ☐No        Money Market Account
☐Yes ☐No        Certificate of Deposits
☐Yes ☐No        Other

## 3) Personal Property

☐Yes ☐No        Antiques
☐Yes ☐No        Jewelry
☐Yes ☐No        Collectibles
☐Yes ☐No        Stamp/Coin & Other Collections
☐Yes ☐No        Other

## 4) Insurance

| | |
|---|---|
| ☐Yes ☐No | Auto |
| ☐Yes ☐No | Homeowners |
| ☐Yes ☐No | Health |
| ☐Yes ☐No | Life |
| ☐Yes ☐No | Long Term Care |
| ☐Yes ☐No | Disability |
| ☐Yes ☐No | Other |

## 5) Real Estate

| | |
|---|---|
| ☐Yes ☐No | Primary Residence |
| ☐Yes ☐No | Rental Property |
| ☐Yes ☐No | Vacation Property |
| ☐Yes ☐No | Vacation Clubs/Timeshares |
| ☐Yes ☐No | Brokerage Accounts |
| ☐Yes ☐No | |

## 6) Business

| | |
|---|---|
| ☐Yes ☐No | Business |

## 7) Investments-Retirement Plans

| | | | |
|---|---|---|---|
| ☐Yes ☐No | 401K | | |
| ☐Yes ☐No | Pension | | |
| ☐Yes ☐No | IRA | ☐Traditional | ☐ROTH |
| ☐Yes ☐No | Profit Sharing | | |
| ☐Yes ☐No | TSA | | |
| ☐Yes ☐No | 403 (B) | | |
| ☐Yes ☐No | PER'S | | |
| ☐Yes ☐No | Military | | |
| ☐Yes ☐No | Other | | |

## 8) Investments-Non-Retirement Plans

☐Yes ☐No     Stocks
☐Yes ☐No     Bonds
☐Yes ☐No     Mutual Funds
☐Yes ☐No     CD's
☐Yes ☐No     Money Market
☐Yes ☐No     Other

## 9) Estate Planning

☐Yes ☐No     Will
☐Yes ☐No     Power of Attorney
☐Yes ☐No     Health Care Directive
☐Yes ☐No     Burial Information
☐Yes ☐No     Trust
☐Yes ☐No     Military
☐Yes ☐No     Other

Notes_____

_____

_____

_____

_____

_____

_____

| Date last revised _____ | Date last revised _____ |
| Date last revised _____ | Date last revised _____ |
| Date last revised _____ | Date last revised _____ |
| Date last revised _____ | Date last revised _____ |

## Section 1

## Personal Information

## & Property

# Estate Organizer

## **Personal Information**

Name_____

Social Security #_____Date of Birth _____

Email_____ Email _____

Tel #_____ Tel #_____

Name_____

Social Security #_____Date of Birth _____

Email_____ Email _____

Tel #_____ Tel #_____

Marital Status
- ☐ Husband & Wife
- ☐ Single
- ☐ Unmarried-Widow/Widower
- ☐ Unmarried-Divorced

Name of Ex _____

Address_____

_____

Tel # _____

Name of Ex _____

Address_____

_____

Tel # _____


(Please include a copy of divorce or separation decrees or agreements at the end or indicate where they are stored)

Do you have a Prenuptial? ☐Yes ☐No    (Please include a copy at the end or indicate where it's stored)

## Citizenship

US Citizenship       ☐Yes ☐No

Other       ☐Yes ☐No _____

US Citizenship       ☐Yes ☐No

Other       ☐Yes ☐No _____

Employment

Are you employed? ☐Yes ☐No    If yes, please continue to answer questions.

Employer _____

Address _____

_____

Contact Name _____ Tel# _____

Are you employed? ☐Yes ☐No    If yes, please continue to answer questions.

Employer _____

Address _____

_____

Contact Name _____ Tel# _____

### Automobiles

Motor Vehicles       ☐Yes ☐No

Make_____Model_____Year_____

Make_____Model_____Year_____

Make_____Model_____Year_____

Make_____Model_____Year_____

See insurance policy section for more details.

## Family Telephone Numbers & Addresses

| | | | |
|---|---|---|---|
| Children | ☐Yes ☐No | #_____ | |
| Step-Children | ☐Yes ☐No | #_____ | |
| Parents Alive | ☐Yes ☐No | #_____ | |

Please provide all information if appropriate.

☐Son   ☐Daughter   ☐Step-Son   ☐Step-Daughter   ☐Parents

Name_____

Address_____

_____

Home Tel# _____ Email _____

Work Tel#_____ Cel#_____

☐Son   ☐Daughter   ☐Step-Son   ☐Step-Daughter   ☐Parents

Name_____

Address_____

_____

Home Tel# _____ Email _____

Work Tel#_____ Cel#_____

☐Son   ☐Daughter   ☐Step-Son   ☐Step-Daughter   ☐Parents

Name_____

Address_____

_____

Home Tel# _____ Email _____

Work Tel#_____ Cel#_____

# Estate Organizer

☐Son  ☐Daughter   ☐Step-Son    ☐Step-Daughter   ☐Parents

Name_____

Address_____

_____

Home Tel# _____ Email _____

Work Tel#_____ Cel#_____


☐Son   ☐Daughter   ☐Step-Son    ☐Step-Daughter   ☐Parents

Name_____

Address_____

_____

Home Tel# _____ Email _____

Work Tel#_____ Cel#_____


☐Son   ☐Daughter   ☐Step-Son    ☐Step-Daughter   ☐Parents

Name_____

Address_____

_____

Home Tel# _____ Email _____

Work Tel#_____ Cel#_____


☐Son   ☐Daughter   ☐Step-Son    ☐Step-Daughter   ☐Parents

Name_____

Address_____

_____

Home Tel# _____ Email _____

Work Tel#_____ Cel#_____

# Estate Organizer

☐Son ☐Daughter ☐Step-Son ☐Step-Daughter ☐Parents

Name_____

Address_____

_____

Home Tel# _____ Email _____

Work Tel#_____ Cel#_____

☐Son ☐Daughter ☐Step-Son ☐Step-Daughter ☐Parents

Name_____

Address_____

_____

Home Tel# _____ Email _____

Work Tel#_____ Cel#_____

☐Son ☐Daughter ☐Step-Son ☐Step-Daughter ☐Parents

Name_____

Address_____

_____

Home Tel# _____ Email _____

Work Tel#_____ Cel#_____

☐Son ☐Daughter ☐Step-Son ☐Step-Daughter ☐Parents

Name_____

Address_____

_____

Home Tel# _____ Email _____

Work Tel#_____ Cel#_____

## Important Professionals Outside the Family

Primary Physician _____

Address _____

_____

Tel # _____ Email _____

Primary Physician _____

Address _____

_____

Tel # _____ Email _____

Specialist Physician _____

Address _____

_____

Tel # _____ Email _____

Specialist Physician _____

Address _____

_____

Tel # _____ Email _____

Specialist Physician _____

Address _____

_____

Tel # _____ Email _____

# Estate Organizer

CPA's Name _____

Address _____

_____

Tel # _____ Email _____

Attorney's Name _____

Address _____

_____

Tel # _____ Email _____

Emergency Contact _____

Address _____

_____

Tel # _____ Email _____

Emergency Contact _____

Address _____

_____

Tel # _____ Email _____

Emergency Contact _____

Address _____

_____

Tel # _____ Email _____

## Medical History

☐Yes ☐No        Heart Disease

☐Yes ☐No        Cancer

☐Yes ☐No        Diabetes

☐Yes ☐No        High Blood Pressure

☐Yes ☐No        High Cholesterol

☐Yes ☐No        Other Medical Issues

Description of Medical Challenges

_____

_____

_____

_____

_____

_____

_____

_____

_____

_____

_____

_____

_____

_____

_____

_____

_____

_____

_____

_____

## Medications

_____

_____

_____

_____

_____

_____

_____

_____

_____

_____

_____

_____

_____

## Medical History

☐Yes ☐No        Heart Disease

☐Yes ☐No        Cancer

☐Yes ☐No        Diabetes

☐Yes ☐No        High Blood Pressure

☐Yes ☐No        High Cholesterol

☐Yes ☐No        Other Medical Issues

Description of Medical Challenges

_____

_____

_____

_____

_____

_____

_____

_____

_____

_____

_____

_____

_____

_____

_____

_____

_____

_____

## Medications

_____

_____

_____

_____

_____

_____

_____

_____

_____

_____

_____

_____

_____

## Other Important Documents

### Birth Certificate

_____

_____

_____

### Marriage Certificate

_____

_____

_____

### Passports

_____

_____

_____

### Warranties

_____

_____

_____

### Other

_____

_____

_____

## Memberships

What memberships do you have?

Golf Club            ☐Yes ☐No
Is it transferable?        ☐Yes ☐No
Description and where is it located?

_____

_____

*(Please include a copy at the end or indicate where it's stored)*

Golf Club            ☐Yes ☐No
Is it transferable?        ☐Yes ☐No
Description and where is it located?

_____

_____

*(Please include a copy at the end or indicate where it's stored)*

Vacation Club/Timeshare        ☐Yes ☐No
Is it transferable?        ☐Yes ☐No
Description and where is it located?

_____

_____

*(Please include a copy at the end or indicate where it's stored)*

Vacation Club/Timeshare        ☐Yes ☐No
Is it transferable?        ☐Yes ☐No
Description and where is it located?

_____

_____

*(Please include a copy at the end or indicate where it's stored)*

## Personal Property

### Antiques

Item_____

_____

_____

Est Value $_____Date Appraised _____

Item_____

_____

_____

Est Value $_____Date Appraised _____

Item_____

_____

_____

Est Value $_____Date Appraised _____

Item_____

_____

_____

Est Value $_____Date Appraised _____

Item_____

_____

_____

Est Value $_____Date Appraised _____

# Estate Organizer

Item_____

_____

_____

Est Value $_____Date Appraised _____

Item_____

_____

_____

Est Value $_____Date Appraised _____

Item_____

_____

_____

Est Value $_____Date Appraised _____

Item_____

_____

_____

Est Value $_____Date Appraised _____

Item_____

_____

_____

Est Value $_____Date Appraised _____

# Estate Organizer

Notes

_____

_____

_____

_____

_____

_____

_____

_____

_____

_____

_____

_____

_____

_____

_____

_____

_____

_____

_____

_____

## Jewelry

Item_____

_____

_____

Est Value $_____ Date Appraised _____

Item_____

_____

_____

Est Value $_____ Date Appraised _____

Item_____

_____

_____

Est Value $_____ Date Appraised _____

Item_____

_____

_____

Est Value $_____ Date Appraised _____

Item_____

_____

_____

Est Value $_____ Date Appraised _____

# Estate Organizer

Item_____

_____

_____

Est Value $_____Date Appraised _____

Item_____

_____

_____

Est Value $_____Date Appraised _____

Item_____

_____

_____

Est Value $_____Date Appraised _____

Item_____

_____

_____

Est Value $_____Date Appraised _____

Notes

_____

_____

_____

_____

_____

## Airline Mileage Plans

Airline_____

Estimated Miles _____


Airline_____

Estimated Miles _____


Airline_____

Estimated Miles _____


Airline_____

Estimated Miles _____


Airline_____

Estimated Miles _____


Airline_____

Estimated Miles _____


Airline_____

Estimated Miles _____


Airline_____

Estimated Miles _____

# Estate Organizer

## Collectibles

Item_____

_____

_____

Est Value $_____ Date Appraised _____


Item_____

_____

_____

Est Value $_____ Date Appraised _____


Item_____

_____

_____

Est Value $_____ Date Appraised _____


Item_____

_____

_____

Est Value $_____ Date Appraised _____


Item_____

_____

_____

Est Value $_____ Date Appraised _____

# Estate Organizer

Item _____

_____

_____

Est Value $_____ Date Appraised _____

Item _____

_____

_____

Est Value $_____ Date Appraised _____

Item _____

_____

_____

Est Value $_____ Date Appraised _____

Notes

_____

_____

_____

_____

_____

_____

_____

_____

_____

# Estate Organizer

## Stamp/Coin or Other Collections

Item_____

_____

_____

Est Value $_____ Date Appraised _____

Item_____

_____

_____

Est Value $_____ Date Appraised _____

Item_____

_____

_____

Est Value $_____ Date Appraised _____

Item_____

_____

_____

Est Value $_____ Date Appraised _____

Item_____

_____

_____

Est Value $_____ Date Appraised _____

## Personal Banking Information

Primary Bank _____

    Whose name is it in?_____

| | | |
|---|---|---|
| Checking | ☐Yes ☐No | Account #_____ |
| Savings | ☐Yes ☐No | Account #_____ |
| Money Market | ☐Yes ☐No | Account #_____ |
| Certificate/Deposits | ☐Yes ☐No | Account #_____ |
| Safety Deposit Box | ☐Yes ☐No | Where is the key?_____ |

Secondary Bank _____

    Whose name is it in?_____

| | | |
|---|---|---|
| Checking | ☐Yes ☐No | Account #_____ |
| Savings | ☐Yes ☐No | Account #_____ |
| Money Market | ☐Yes ☐No | Account #_____ |
| Certificate/Deposits | ☐Yes ☐No | Account #_____ |
| Safety Deposit Box | ☐Yes ☐No | Where is the key?_____ |

Secondary Bank _____

    Whose name is it in?_____

| | | |
|---|---|---|
| Checking | ☐Yes ☐No | Account #_____ |
| Savings | ☐Yes ☐No | Account #_____ |
| Money Market | ☐Yes ☐No | Account #_____ |
| Certificate/Deposits | ☐Yes ☐No | Account #_____ |
| Safety Deposit Box | ☐Yes ☐No | Where is the key?_____ |

_____

_____

_____

## Personal Credit Card Information

If you need more credit card space, please copy this page before filling out to provide adequate space for your needs

Credit Card _____Exp Date_____

Account Number_____

Contact Information _____


Credit Card _____Exp Date_____

Account Number_____

Contact Information _____


Credit Card _____Exp Date_____

Account Number_____

Contact Information _____


Credit Card _____Exp Date_____

Account Number_____

Contact Information _____


Credit Card _____Exp Date_____

Account Number_____

Contact Information _____

# Estate Organizer

Credit Card _____ Exp Date_____

Account Number_____

Contact Information _____


Credit Card _____ Exp Date_____

Account Number_____

Contact Information _____


Credit Card _____ Exp Date_____

Account Number_____

Contact Information _____


Credit Card _____ Exp Date_____

Account Number_____

Contact Information _____


Credit Card _____ Exp Date_____

Account Number_____

Contact Information _____


Credit Card _____ Exp Date_____

Account Number_____

Contact Information _____

Securities and advisory services offered through Centaurus Financial Inc., a registered broker-dealer and investment advisor.
Member FINRA /SIPC Northwest Financial Solutions and Centaurus Financial, Inc. are not affiliated companies.

Notes

_____

_____

_____

_____

_____

_____

_____

_____

_____

_____

_____

_____

_____

_____

_____

_____

_____

_____

_____

_____

_____

## Section 2

## Insurance Policies

## Auto

Do you have an Automobile?    ☐Yes ☐No   How many?_____

Make_____Model_____Year_____

Make_____Model_____Year_____

Make_____Model_____Year_____

Make_____Model_____Year_____

Make_____Model_____Year_____

Insurance Agent's Name_____

Company_____

Address_____

_____

Tel #_____Policy #_____

## Recreation Vehicle    ☐Yes ☐No

Make_____Model_____Year_____

Company_____

Address_____

_____

Tel #_____Policy #_____

# Estate Organizer

## Boat             ☐Yes ☐No

Make_____Model_____Year_____

Company_____

Address_____

_____

Tel #_____Policy #_____

## Other             ☐Yes ☐No

Make_____Model_____Year_____

Company_____

Address_____

_____

Tel #_____Policy#_____

## Other             ☐Yes ☐No

Make_____Model_____Year_____

Company_____

Address_____

_____

Tel #_____Policy #_____

Notes _____

_____

_____

# Estate Organizer

## Homeowners Insurance

Do you own your home? ☐Yes ☐No

Are you buying your home? ☐Yes ☐No

Insurance Agent's Name_____

Company_____

Address_____

_____

Tel #_____Policy #_____


Do you have Mortgage Insurance? ☐Yes ☐No

Insurance Agents Name_____

Company_____

Address_____

_____

Tel #_____Policy #_____


## Liability Umbrella

Do you have Liability Umbrella? ☐Yes ☐No

Insurance Agents Name_____

Company_____

Address_____

_____

Tel #_____Policy #_____


Notes_____

_____

_____

## Life Insurance

Name of Insured_____

Insurance Agents Name_____

Company_____

Address_____

Tel #_____Policy #_____

Policy #_____Death Benefit $_____

Beneficiary_____ Last Updated_____

Name of Insured_____

Insurance Agents Name_____

Company_____

Address_____

Tel #_____Policy #_____

Policy #_____Death Benefit $_____

Beneficiary_____ Last Updated_____

Notes_____

_____

_____

_____

_____

_____

_____

_____

# Estate Organizer

## Life Insurance

Insurance Agents Name_____

Company_____

Address_____

Tel #_____ Policy #_____

Policy #_____ Death Benefit $_____

Beneficiary_____ Last Updated_____

Name of Insured_____

Insurance Agents Name_____

Company_____

Address_____

Tel #_____ Policy #_____

Policy #_____ Death Benefit $_____

Beneficiary_____ Last Updated_____

Notes_____

_____

_____

_____

_____

_____

_____

_____

_____

## Health Insurance

Do you have Health Insurance? ☐Yes ☐No

Insurance Agents Name_____

Company_____

Address_____

Tel #_____Policy #_____


Do you have Health Insurance? ☐Yes ☐No

Insurance Agents Name_____

Company_____

Address_____

Tel #_____Policy #_____


Do you have Health Supplemental Insurance?      ☐Yes ☐No

Insurance Agents Name_____

Company_____

Address_____

Tel #_____Policy #_____


Do you have Health Supplemental Insurance?      ☐Yes ☐No

Insurance Agents Name_____

Company_____

Address_____

Tel #_____Policy #_____

## Dental Insurance

Do you have Dental Insurance? ☐Yes ☐No

Insurance Agents Name_____

Company_____

Address_____

_____

Tel #_____Policy #_____


Do you have Dental Insurance? ☐Yes ☐No

Insurance Agents Name_____

Company_____

Address_____

Tel #_____Policy #_____


Notes_____

_____

_____

_____

_____

_____

_____

_____

_____

_____

## Vision Insurance

Do you have Vision Insurance?          ☐Yes ☐No

Insurance Agents Name_____

Company_____

Address_____

Tel #_____Policy #_____


Do you have Vision Insurance?          ☐Yes ☐No

Insurance Agents Name_____

Company_____

Address_____

Tel #_____Policy #_____


Notes_____

_____

_____

_____

_____

_____

_____

_____

_____

_____

## Long Term Care

Name of Insured_____

Insurance Agents Name_____

Company_____

Address_____

Tel #_____Policy #_____


Name of Insured_____

Insurance Agents Name_____

Company_____

Address_____

Tel #_____Policy #_____


Notes_____

_____

_____

_____

_____

_____

_____

_____

_____

_____

## Disability Insurance

Name of Insured_____

Insurance Agents Name_____

Company_____

Address_____

Tel #_____Policy #_____


Name of Insured_____

Insurance Agents Name_____

Company_____

Address_____

Tel #_____Policy #_____


Notes_____

_____

_____

_____

_____

_____

_____

_____

_____

_____

_____

## Supplemental Insurance

Name of Insured_____

Insurance Agents Name_____

Company_____

Address_____

Tel #_____Policy #_____


Name of Insured_____

Insurance Agents Name_____

Company_____

Address_____

Tel #_____Policy #_____


Name of Insured_____

Insurance Agents Name_____

Company_____

Address_____

Tel #_____Policy #_____


Name of Insured_____

Insurance Agents Name_____

Company_____

Address_____

Tel #_____Policy #_____

# Section 3

# Business

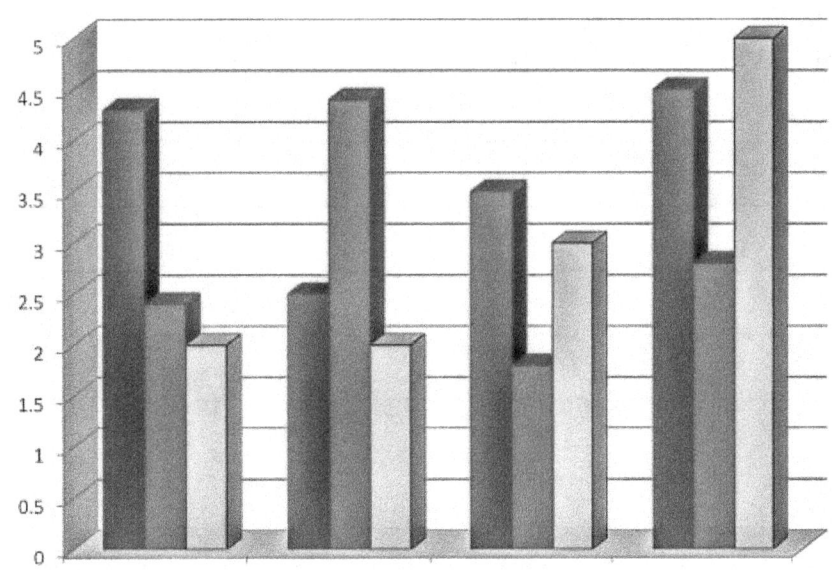

## Business Information

Do you have a business? ☐Yes ☐No   If yes, please continue to answer questions.

Name of Business_____

Address_____

_____

Tel#_____Fax_____

Website _____Email _____

    Sole Proprietor    ☐Yes ☐No
    Partnership    ☐Yes ☐No

Name of Partner_____

Address_____

_____

Contact Tel #_____

Cel #_____


Name of Partner_____

Address_____

_____

Contact Tel #_____

Cel #_____

# Estate Organizer

Name of Partner_____

Address_____

_____

Contact Tel #_____

Cel #_____


Name of Partner_____

Address_____

_____

Contact Tel #_____

Cel #_____


Corporation         ☐Yes ☐No

Board of Directors

Board Member_____

Address_____

_____

Contact Tel #_____

Cel #_____


Board Member_____

Address_____

_____

Contact Tel #_____

Cel #_____

# Estate Organizer

Board Member_____

Address_____

_____

Contact Tel #_____

Cel #_____


Board Member_____

Address_____

_____

Contact Tel #_____

Cel #_____


Board Member_____

Address_____

_____

Contact Tel #_____

Cel #_____


Board Member_____

Address_____

_____

Contact Tel #_____

Cel #_____


Board Member_____

Address_____

_____

Contact Tel #_____

Cel #_____

## Business Banking

Primary Bank_____

    Whose name is it in?_____

    Checking             ☐Yes ☐No

    Account #_____

    Savings              ☐Yes ☐No

    Account #_____

    Money Market      ☐Yes ☐No

    Account #_____

    Certificate/Deposits  ☐Yes ☐No

    Account #_____

    Safety Deposit Box   ☐Yes ☐No   Where is the key?_____

    Notes_____

_____

_____

_____

_____

_____

_____

_____

_____

_____

# Estate Organizer

Secondary Bank_____

    Whose name is it in?_____

    Checking           ☐Yes ☐No

    Account #_____

    Savings            ☐Yes ☐No

    Account #_____

    Money Market     ☐Yes ☐No

    Account #_____

    Certificate/Deposits  ☐Yes ☐No

    Account #_____

    Safety Deposit Box   ☐Yes ☐No

    Where is the key? _____

Notes_____

_____

_____

_____

_____

_____

_____

_____

_____

_____

_____

## Business Credit Cards

Credit Card _____ Exp Date _____

Account Number _____

Contact Information _____


Credit Card _____ Exp Date _____

Account Number _____

Contact Information _____


Credit Card _____ Exp Date _____

Account Number _____

Contact Information _____


Credit Card _____ Exp Date _____

Account Number _____

Contact Information _____


Credit Card _____ Exp Date _____

Account Number _____

Contact Information _____


Credit Card _____ Exp Date _____

Account Number _____

Contact Information _____

## Important People in the Business

### Bookkeeper

Name_____

Address_____

_____

Home Tel #_____

Work Tel #_____Cel#_____

Email_____

### CPA –Accountant

Name_____

Address_____

_____

Home Tel #_____

Work Tel #_____Cel#_____

Email_____

### Office Manager

Name_____

Address_____

_____

Home Tel #_____

Work Tel #_____Cel#_____

Email_____

# Estate Organizer

## Secretary

Name_____

Address_____

_____

Home Tel #_____

Work Tel #_____Cel#_____

Email_____

## Executive Assistant

Name_____

Address_____

_____

Home Tel #_____

Work Tel #_____Cel#_____

Email_____

## Attorney

Name_____

Address_____

_____

Home Tel #_____

Work Tel #_____Cel#_____

Email_____

# Estate Organizer

## Attorney

Name_____

Address_____

_____

Home Tel #_____

Work Tel #_____Cel#_____

Email_____

## Other Emergency Contacts

Name_____

Address_____

_____

Home Tel #_____

Work Tel #_____Cel#_____

Email_____

## Other Emergency Contacts

Name_____

Address_____

_____

Home Tel #_____

Work Tel #_____Cel#_____

Email_____

# Section 4

# Investments

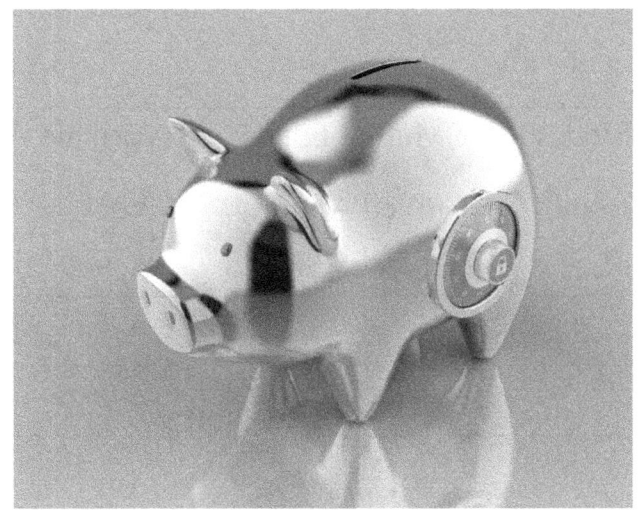

## Investments-Retirement Plans

If you have more investment options, please copy this page before filling out to provide adequate space for your needs.

| | | | |
|---|---|---|---|
| 401K | ☐Yes ☐No | TSA | ☐Yes ☐No |
| Pension | ☐Yes ☐No | 403 (B) | ☐Yes ☐No |
| Traditional IRA | ☐Yes ☐No | PER'S | ☐Yes ☐No |
| ROTH IRA | ☐Yes ☐No | Military | ☐Yes ☐No |
| Profit Sharing | ☐Yes ☐No | Other | ☐Yes ☐No |

## 401K

Owners Name _____

   Product Type   ☐Stocks   ☐Mutual Funds   ☐Variable Annuity

                  ☐Bonds   ☐Fixed Annuity   ☐Other

Company_____

Tel #_____ Email_____

Policy #_____ Est Value $ _____

Owners Name _____

   Product Type   ☐Stocks   ☐Mutual Funds   ☐Variable Annuity

                  ☐Bonds   ☐Fixed Annuity   ☐Other

Company_____

Tel #_____ Email_____

Policy #_____ Est Value $ _____

# Estate Organizer

## 401K

Owners Name _____

    Product Type   ☐Stocks     ☐Mutual Funds     ☐Variable Annuity

                   ☐Bonds     ☐Fixed Annuity     ☐Other

Company_____

Tel #_____ Email_____

Policy #_____Est Value $ _____

Owners Name _____

    Product Type   ☐Stocks     ☐Mutual Funds     ☐Variable Annuity

                   ☐Bonds     ☐Fixed Annuity     ☐Other

Company_____

Tel #_____ Email_____

Policy #_____Est Value $ _____

Notes_____

_____

_____

_____

_____

_____

_____

_____

_____

## Pension

Owners Name _____

Company _____

Tel #_____ Emails _____

Policy #_____ Est Value $_____


Owners Name _____

Company _____

Tel #_____ Emails _____

Policy #_____ Est Value $_____

## IRA-Traditional or Roth

Owners Name _____

Company _____

Tel #_____ Emails _____

Policy #_____ Est Value $_____


Owners Name _____

Company _____

Tel #_____ Emails _____

Policy #_____ Est Value $_____

Notes_____

_____

_____

Securities and advisory services offered through Centaurus Financial Inc., a registered broker-dealer and investment advisor.
Member FINRA /SIPC Northwest Financial Solutions and Centaurus Financial, Inc. are not affiliated companies.

# Estate Organizer

## TSA

Owners Name _____

Company_____

Tel #_____ Emails_____

Policy #_____ Est Value $_____

Owners Name _____

Company_____

Tel #_____ Emails_____

Policy #_____ Est Value $_____

## 403 (B)

Owners Name _____

Company_____

Tel #_____ Emails_____

Policy #_____ Est Value $_____

Owners Name _____

Company_____

Tel #_____ Emails_____

Policy #_____ Est Value $_____

Notes_____

_____

_____

_____

## PER'S

Owners Name_____

Company_____

Tel #_____Emails_____

Policy #_____Est Value $_____


Owners Name _____

Company_____

Tel #_____Emails_____

Policy #_____Est Value $_____

## Military

Owners Name _____

Branch of Service_____Rank_____

Military Benefits      ☐Yes ☐No


Owners Name _____

Branch of Service_____Rank_____

Military Benefits      ☐Yes ☐No


Notes_____

_____

_____

_____

## Investments-Non Retirement Plans

If you have more investment options, please copy this page before filling out to provide adequate space for your needs.

Stocks      ☐Yes ☐No       C D's       ☐Yes ☐No
Bonds      ☐Yes ☐No       Money Market       ☐Yes ☐No
Mutual Funds      ☐Yes ☐No

Owners Name _____

    Product Type   ☐Stocks     ☐Bonds     ☐Mutual Funds
                   ☐CD's     ☐Money Market   ☐Other

Stock/Fund Name_____

Brokers Name_____

Tel # _____Email_____

Company _____Est Value $_____

Owners Name _____

    Product Type   ☐Stocks     ☐Bonds     ☐Mutual Funds
                   ☐CD's     ☐Money Market   ☐Other

Stock/Fund Name_____

Brokers Name_____

Tel # _____Email_____

Company _____Est Value $_____

Notes_____

_____

_____

# Estate Organizer

Owners Name _____

    Product Type   ☐Stocks   ☐Bonds   ☐Mutual Funds

                      ☐CD's   ☐Money Market   ☐Other

Stock/Fund Name_____

Brokers Name _____

Tel # _____Email_____

Company _____Est Value $_____

Owners Name _____

    Product Type   ☐Stocks   ☐Bonds   ☐Mutual Funds

                      ☐CD's   ☐Money Market   ☐Other

Stock/Fund Name_____

Brokers Name_____

Tel # _____Email_____

Company _____Est Value $_____

Owners Name _____

    Product Type   ☐Stocks   ☐Bonds   ☐Mutual Funds

                      ☐CD's   ☐Money Market   ☐Other

Stock/Fund Name_____

Brokers Name_____

Tel # _____Email_____

Company _____Est Value $_____

Notes_____

_____

_____

# Estate Organizer

Owners Name _____

    Product Type   ☐Stocks    ☐Bonds    ☐Mutual Funds
                ☐CD's     ☐Money Market  ☐Other

Stock/Fund Name_____

Brokers Name_____

Tel # _____Email_____

Company _____Est Value $_____

Owners Name _____

    Product Type   ☐Stocks    ☐Bonds    ☐Mutual Funds
                ☐CD's     ☐Money Market  ☐Other

Stock/Fund Name_____

Brokers Name_____

Tel # _____Email_____

Company _____Est Value $_____

Owners Name _____

    Product Type   ☐Stocks    ☐Bonds    ☐Mutual Funds
                ☐CD's     ☐Money Market  ☐Other

Stock/Fund Name_____

Brokers Name_____

Tel # _____Email_____

Company _____Est Value $_____

Notes_____

_____

_____

# Estate Organizer

## Real Estate Investments

If you have more real estate options, please copy this page before filling out. This will provide adequate space for your needs.

☐Primary Residence ☐Rental Home ☐Vacation Home ☐Other

Address_____

_____

Mortgage Holder_____

Address_____

_____

Tel #_____ Email _____

Account #_____ Est Value $_____


☐Primary Residence ☐Rental Home ☐Vacation Home ☐Other

Address_____

_____

Mortgage Holder_____

Address_____

_____

Tel #_____ Email _____

Account #_____ Est Value $_____


Notes_____

_____

_____

_____

Securities and advisory services offered through Centaurus Financial Inc., a registered broker-dealer and investment advisor. Member FINRA /SIPC Northwest Financial Solutions and Centaurus Financial, Inc. are not affiliated companies.

## Real Estate Investments

☐Primary Residence     ☐Rental Home     ☐Vacation Home   ☐Other

Address_____

_____

Mortgage Holder_____

Address_____

_____

Tel #_____Email _____

Account #_____Est Value $_____


☐Primary Residence  ☐Rental Home     ☐Vacation Home   ☐Other

Address_____

_____

Mortgage Holder_____

Address_____

_____

Tel #_____Email _____

Account #_____Est Value $_____


Notes_____

_____

_____

_____

_____

## Estate Planning

Will

Do you have a will?      ☐Yes ☐No   Last updated_____
   Who is the executor?

Name_____

Address_____

_____

Tel #_____Email_____


Who is the alternative executor?
   Name_____

Address_____

_____

Tel #_____Email_____

(Please include copy at the end or indicate where it's stored)


Notes_____

_____

_____

_____

_____

_____

_____

_____

Securities and advisory services offered through Centaurus Financial Inc., a registered broker-dealer and investment advisor.
Member FINRA /SIPC Northwest Financial Solutions and Centaurus Financial, Inc. are not affiliated companies.

## Power of Attorney

Do you have a power of attorney?　　☐Yes ☐No　Last updated_____

Who is named_____

　Address_____

　_____

　Tel #_____Email_____

　(Please include copy at the end or indicate where it's stored)

_____

_____

_____

_____

_____

## Health Care Directive

Do you have a Health Directive?　　☐Yes ☐No　Last updated_____
　(Please include copy at the end or indicate where it's stored)

_____

_____

_____

_____

_____

_____

_____

## Burial Information

Have you made plans for your burial/cremation?     ☐Yes ☐No

Funeral Home _____

Address_____

_____

Tel # _____

Cemetery _____

(Please include copy at the end or indicate where it's stored)

_____

_____

_____

Have you made plans for your burial/cremation?     ☐Yes ☐No

Funeral Home _____

Address_____

_____

Tel # _____

Cemetery _____

(Please include copy at the end or indicate where it's stored)

_____

_____

_____

_____

## Trust

Do you have a Living Trust?           ☐Yes ☐No        Last updated_____

Do you have any other kind of Trust? ☐Yes ☐No        Last updated_____

Who is the trustee?

Name_____

Address_____

_____

Tel #_____Email_____

Who is the alternative trustee?

Name_____

Address_____

_____

Tel #_____Email_____

 (Please include copy at the end or indicate where it's stored)

Notes

_____

_____

_____

_____

_____

_____

## Important Telephone Numbers
## to Navigate the System

Aging ----------------------------------------------------------------------------------http://aoa.gov

Compassionate Friends------------------------------------------------- 877-969-0010

www.compassionatefriends.org

Eldercare------------------------------------------------------------------- 800-677-1116

www.eldercare.gov

Hospice--------------------------------------------------------------------- 800-854-3402

www.hospicefoundation.org

Internal Revenue Service -------------------------------------------------800-829-1040

TTY------------------------------------------------------------------- 800-829-4059

http://www.irs.gov

Medicare -------------------------------------------------------------------800-633-4227

www.medicare.gov

Medicaid-------------------------------------------------------------------- 877-267-2323

www.cms.hhs.gov/medicaid

Social Security Office--------------------------------------------------------- 800-772-1213

TTY------------------------------------------------------------------------- 800-325-0778

www.ssa.gov

www.socialsecurity.gov

VA (Federal) Benefit Info & Claims-------------------------------------- 800-827-1000

www.va.gov

www.vba.va.gov/survivors/

## Other Important People to Notify

Name_____

Address_____

Home Tel#_____

Work Tel#_____Cel#_____

Email_____

Name_____

Address_____

Home Tel#_____

Work Tel#_____Cel#_____

Email_____

Name_____

Address_____

Home Tel#_____

Work Tel#_____Cel#_____

Email_____

Name_____

Address_____

Home Tel#_____

Work Tel#_____Cel#_____

Email_____

## Other Important People to Notify

Name_____

Address_____

Home Tel#_____

Work Tel#_____Cel#_____

Email_____


Name_____

Address_____

Home Tel#_____

Work Tel#_____Cel#_____

Email_____


Name_____

Address_____

Home Tel#_____

Work Tel#_____Cel#_____

Email_____


Name_____

Address_____

Home Tel#_____

Work Tel#_____Cel#_____

Email_____

# Estate Organizer

Notes_____

_____

_____

_____

_____

_____

_____

_____

_____

_____

_____

_____

_____

_____

_____

_____

_____

_____

_____

_____

_____

_____

_____

_____

_____

_____

_____

_____

_____

_____

_____

_____

_____

_____

_____

_____

_____

_____

_____

_____

_____

_____

_____

_____

_____

_____

_____

_____

_____

_____

_____

_____

_____

_____

_____

_____

_____

_____

_____

_____

_____

_____

_____

_____

_____

_____

_____

_____

_____

_____

_____

_____

_____

_____

_____

_____

_____

Example Letter

Date:_____

As we know life is short and things happen. I have attempted to compile a comprehensive overview of my life including important documents you might need if something were to happen. I wanted to make things as easy as possible for the people I leave behind.

The Simple Life Organizer is equipped with four sections by topics.

1. **Personal Information:** This section includes many things you may already know but some you do not. It includes important telephone numbers and addresses, medical information and credit card information. It includes personal property includes antiques, collections and art. It also includes personal banking with account numbers and safety deposit information. Other personal items like timeshares and any membership ie, golf clubs, travel clubs.
2. **Insurance Policy Info:** This section includes all the insurance policies I have including life, health, auto, long term care & disability.
3. **Business:** If I have a business, this section includes an overview of business relationships, bank accounts, and important telephone numbers.
4. **Investments:** This section includes both retirement and non-retirement type of investments with account numbers and contact names. It also includes real estate investments like primary residence, rentals and vacation homes. It also itemizes estate plan including my will, trust info, power of attorney, and health directives.

I have assembled many of my pertinent telephone numbers, important papers, and wishes in case something happens to me and you will need access to this information. I will be storing this book

_____.

Passwords and security codes are kept separate for additional security, they can be found

_____.

For updated information that may not be contained in this book, please contact my CPA, Attorney and/or Investment Advisor for more details

Sincerely, _____

Securities and advisory services offered through Centaurus Financial Inc., a registered broker-dealer and investment advisor. Member FINRA /SIPC Northwest Financial Solutions and Centaurus Financial, Inc. are not affiliated companies.